Burn
Pythons

Plus Reticulated Pythons and Related Species

FROM THE EXPERTS AT
ADVANCED VIVARIUM SYSTEMS®

By Philippe de Vosjoli
with Roger Klingenberg, DVM

THE HERPETOCULTURAL LIBRARY®
Advanced Vivarium Systems®
Irvine, California

Jarelle S. Stein, *Editor*
Indexed by Rachel Rice

Cover image by Paul Freed.
The additional photographs in this book are by James Gerholdt, pp. 6, 7; Isabelle Francias, p. 21 (bottom); Paul Freed, pp. 10, 15, 17, 21 (top), 22, 25, 26, 29, 30, 35, 37, 39, 44, 58, 64–67, 70, 72; Roger Klingenberg, 24, 52, 54, 55; Bill Love, 62, 73; Maleta M. Walls, 18, 47, 48, 50.

LCCN: 96-183295
ISBN 13: 978-1-882770-83-0

An Imprint of BowTie Press®
A Division of BowTie, Inc.
3 Burroughs
Irvine, CA 92618
www.avsbooks.com

We want to hear from you. What books would you like to see in the future? Please feel free to write us with any comments on our AVS books.

Printed in Singapore
10 9 8 7 6 5 4 3 2

CONTENTS

ACKNOWLEDGMENTS

A tip of the herper hat goes to Bob Clark, who single-handedly was responsible for establishing most of the morphs of Burmese pythons and reticulated pythons in captivity, and whose articles provided essential information for this book. His pythons represent supreme examples of living art. Special thanks are due to Ernie Wagner of Seattle, Wash., who reviewed the original 1991 manuscript and provided valuable advice.

BEFORE BUYING A BURMESE PYTHON

During the early 1970s, the author was fortunate in obtaining a hatchling Burmese python that in time grew into an impressive 12-foot (3.7-meter) snake with an outstandingly docile temperament. Of all the snakes that the author has owned, none has ever equaled this particular animal in terms of personality and responsiveness. This Burmese python eventually appeared in a number of newspaper articles, in herpetological shows, and in several classroom and school presentations on amphibians and reptiles. This special animal performed innumerable services in helping to dispel myths and popular misconceptions about snakes, tolerating at times more than a dozen little hands trying to feel the skin of a living giant snake.

Beauty, slow movement, heavy body proportion, calm disposition, and a greater degree of responsiveness than demonstrated by most other snake species have made the Burmese python a favorite among those seeking to own a snake pet. Yet Burmese pythons are in several ways far from the ideal pet snake. In spite of the docile personality of many specimens (this may depend on genetics as well as frequency and quality of interaction), the fact is that Burmese pythons usually grow into large, heavy, powerful predators that have feeding, housing, and handling requirements that make them unsuitable as pets for many members of the general public. Just as with certain dog breeds, Burmese pythons are not recommended for everyone.

Today, with the rapid advances in herpetoculture, increasing numbers of captive-bred Burmese pythons are purchased by budding herpetoculturists as snake pets. The growing popularity of Burmese pythons is at one level an indication of a slowly growing change of attitude by the general population toward reptiles and reptile-keeping. At another level, the keeping of large snakes by members of the general population has become a concern of certain states, cities, and townships that question the wisdom of allowing private individuals to keep what they consider "potentially dangerous" large constrictors. The result has been the numerous legislative proposals put forth to various agencies every year in an attempt to restrict herpetoculturists from keeping large snakes.

The albino trait, shown in this Burmese python, can be combined with other traits such as patternless and labyrinth.

Evaluate Your Choices

Many people who buy Burmese pythons probably should not. They have no clear notion of the difference between the small hatchling that can be held in one hand and be housed in a 10-gallon (38-liter) vivarium, and the large adult that may require two people for handling and require a cage that will take up a significant portion of a room. Most first-time Burmese python buyers also don't fully grasp the fact that they will start by feeding their baby snake a mouse and end up with having to feed it large rabbits.

If you want a large snake, there are other species that don't grow quite as large and are easier to handle as adults, such as boa constrictors (*Boa constrictor*), Dumeril's boas (*Acrantophis dumerili*), rainbow boas (*Epicrates cenchria*), ball pythons (*Python regius*), and carpet pythons (*Morelia spilota*). Granted, Burmese pythons also have great qualities: large and impressive sizes, beauty, and many (when captive-

Large snakes require large prey. While you'll start out feeding a hatchling Burmese small mice, an adult specimen will require larger prey; for instance, large rats or rabbits.

raised from juveniles) have about the nicest personalities you can find in snakes. But is a giant snake really what you want?

This type of decision is no different from the one that confronts a dog buyer. Before purchasing a snake, consider your lifestyle, such as whether you live in an apartment or a large home, whether children are in the home, how much free time is available, and the ease of obtaining required food items; finally, consider selection of the proper species. Is the Burmese python going to end up in your studio apartment or in a special room on the bottom floor of the house? Are your young children likely to tamper with it? If you're an older person, will you be able to handle the adult animal when it exceeds 60 pounds (27 kilograms) in weight? Will there be someone there to help you? These are the things you should think about if you intend to be a responsible snake owner.

Being a Responsible Snake Owner

Each year, hundreds of pet snakes in the United States escape from their inadequate cages. Many are never found by their owners. Others end up making the news, including many escapee large constrictors (the state of Florida seems to be number one on the list of reported escaped large constrictors). Every time this happens, it fuels those who are opposed to the keeping of exotic animals, including large constrictors, by the private sector. In addition, bad publicity is caused by individuals who take their snakes out in public places (outside of the proper forum for such displays) and by individuals who intentionally aim to shock people. News media love incidents that involve reptiles. The public subconsciously must look forward to these incidents, as they give them something to talk about without even having to read the *National Enquirer.*

The now defunct but once pioneering American Federation of Herpetoculturists (AFH) years ago established guidelines for the responsible keeping of large constrictors. These guidelines have been presented at several public hearings and served as models for sound regulation. An updated version of the guidelines follows:

- In consideration of the right of the public to not unexpectedly be exposed to snakes such as large constrictors, and realizing the irresponsible behaviors demonstrated by some snake owners, it is recommended that no snake shall be openly displayed in a public setting outside of proper and established forums, such as herpetological shows, educational displays, pet stores, and events whereby members of the public are forewarned that snakes may be openly displayed.
- All large snakes must be housed in secure enclosures with either hinged doors, sliding tops, or sliding glass fronts that include a locking mechanism. Such enclosures should preferably be contained in a room modified to prevent snake escapes and with a door that shall be kept shut or locked when the room is not occupied by the owners. As herpetoculturists, we all benefit from practices that prevent the escape of pet snakes.
- All snakes must be transported in a manner that prevents the possibility of escape. They shall be contained in a sturdy cloth bag free of holes or tears and placed inside a box or similar container with holes for aeration. The container should then be sealed or locked shut. Care must be taken to use cloth bags with a weave that allows for adequate air exchange. When shipping

snakes by air, the airlines must be consulted as to their packing requirements.

- When handling or performing maintenance of any of the giant snakes more than 8 feet (2.4 m) (green anacondas, Asian rock pythons including Burmese pythons, African rock pythons, reticulated pythons, and scrub pythons), another person should be present or at least within easy calling range. An additional person should be present for every additional 4 feet (1.2 m) of snake, i.e., two people when handling or maintaining a 12-foot (3.7-m) python.
- No boids (pythons and boas) that can achieve an adult length more than 8 feet (2.4 m) should ever be owned by or sold to minors.
- As with other potentially dangerous animals, such as dogs, owners of large constrictors should be aware that they can be liable for the medical costs of treating injuries as well as additional financial damages.

Be Responsible—Preserve Our Hobby

Between Jan 1, 2000 and Jan 1, 2005, there were more than thirty-six news reports relating to escaped large pythons. These reports are compiled by anti-herpetoculture organizations (Humane Society of the United States, Animal Protection Institute, etc.) and used as arguments to support legislation that would remove our rights to keep and breed reptiles. Only responsible pet-keeping, self-regulation by the pet industry and by the private sector, support of pro-pet organizations such as the Pet Industry Joint Advisory Council (PIJAC), and involvement in related politics can prevent the steady creep of legislative restrictions.

Regulations

There appears to have been a trend in the last few years for cities and states to draft ordinances or regulations that control or restrict ownership of large snakes. Various agencies and organizations directly or indirectly support these regulations, particularly with regard to the ownership of large constrictors (typically boas and pythons that can achieve an

Although reported snake-related deaths are few, cities across the United States have drafted regulations that control or outlaw the keeping of large constrictors. Practicing responsible herpetoculture will help educate the public that these large snakes are no more dangerous than are dogs and cats.

adult length of more than 8 feet [2.4 m]). Those opposed to large snake-keeping contend that the public should be protected from the remote possibility of danger from these animals. Most of these proposed regulations conceal the underlying persistent bias against snakes that to this day permeates the attitudes of many people.

One would assume from these regulations that potentially dangerous things should not, as a matter of course, be possessed by the general public. One could also be led to believe that these various agencies look out for our welfare. In fact, our lives are routinely affected by much greater probabilities of danger than presented by large constrictors, and these dangers are condoned by numerous agencies as well as the federal government. Dogs raised and kept by irresponsible owners are clearly dangerous, as statistical data indicate (ten to fifteen deaths per year and millions of dollars spent in treating bites). Cats can be dangerous. They can claw (many people don't seem to mind); they account for a significant percentage of reported animal bites; and they can carry some nasty diseases. Living near other humans can be very dangerous. In fact, based on available statistics, a human has a far greater chance of being seriously injured from a bite by a fellow human than by a large constrictor.

The cars we drive are potentially dangerous, as several thousand deaths every year indicate. So is ownership of guns. Horses, if one were to look at available data in the

United States, are one of the most dangerous of domestic animals and many times more dangerous than snakes in terms of deaths and accidents. The electrical appliances in our homes are dangerous, as is the use of natural gas. So are drinking alcohol and smoking.

In the midst of such numerous potential dangers that are an intrinsic part of life, poorly informed and biased state and local agencies regularly propose laws and ordinances that would attempt to ban ownership of large constrictors. If they relied on hard data rather than prejudice, they could make a much better case for banning ownership of dogs, guns, automobiles, horses, toasters, cocktails, and so on.

In the case of Burmese pythons, what becomes evident is that they have an extremely low behavioral propensity to kill humans by constriction. In one report that investigated authenticated deaths by large constrictors in the United States between 1978 and 1988, four deaths were reported, of which three were caused by reticulated pythons and one involved a Burmese python. Furthermore, at least three of the cases involved irresponsible herpetocultural practices. Considering the many large constrictors, including tens of thousands of Burmese pythons, that were imported and sold during that period, and considering the much more threatening dangers that are generally accepted as a normal part of everyday life, the potential danger presented by large constrictors pales. It is worth noting, however, that between 1999 and 2004, deaths by large pythons in the United States have averaged about one per year, involving mostly young adult Burmese pythons (see Ontogeny section, Stage 2, in the Burmese Python Basics chapter). All of these deaths resulted from ignorance or failure to practice proper herpetocultural procedures.

With a minimum of common sense and by adopting the recommendations made by herpetological organizations such as the AFH, any problems associated with the ownership of large snakes can be addressed in a responsible manner without perpetuating bias and misinformation and without threatening the rights of herpetoculturists to practice their avocation.

Nonetheless, before purchasing a Burmese python or any other large constrictor, check your state, county, and local regulations for any provisions applying to the ownership of reptiles by individuals. Besides contacting the agencies in charge of implementing these regulations, other good sources of information are local herpetological societies. (Updated lists of societies are available at http://www.kingsnake.com and at http://www.reptilesmagazine.com.) It does not pay to break the law in this particular area. Before you know it, you could be making newspaper headlines and the six o'clock news. If local authorities call in the state or federal enforcement agencies (state fish and game departments and the U.S. Fish and Wildlife Service) to investigate the possibility of other violations, you could also have an experience of personal violation that you are not about to forget. In some areas, possible possession of an illegal reptile can get more media attention than a major drug bust.

CHAPTER 1

BURMESE PYTHON BASICS

Today, the Burmese python is one of the most commonly sold snakes as well as one of the most beautiful in its varied color morphs. Once a standard prop of carnival snake charmers and dancers, today it is more likely to be seen on display in zoos and nature centers and drawing attention in pet shops. Its large size and great bulk when fully mature never fail to attract attention, helping make it a popular but dangerous pet. In nature it is slow to move and largely sedentary, adults lying in wait near game trails to grab mammals, birds, and reptiles. They are most likely to be found near bodies of water in rain forests because water helps support the weight of the adult snake, but they are far from helpless on land and can climb trees with ease, using the prehensile tail for balance. Though substantiated reports of wild Burmese pythons killing humans are rare, this actually has happened, the victims usually being children or adults of small stature.

Scientific Name

The scientific name of the Burmese python is *Python molurus bivittatus*. It is a subspecies of the Asiatic rock python, *P. molurus*.

Distribution

The Burmese python is native throughout the Indo-Chinese subregion including Borneo, southern China, Hainan, Hong Kong, Java, Myanmar (Burma), Sulawesi (Celebes), Sumbawa, Thailand, and Vietnam. The great majority of the those first established in captivity in the United States originated from Thailand, but in recent years imports have been brought in from Vietnam and Indonesia, including new and unusual morphs such as dwarf Burmese pythons. Burmese pythons are now protected in Thailand; consequently, relatively few wild-collected Burmese from there are being imported into the United States.

Protection

All pythons and boas, including the Burmese python, are considered threatened by the Convention on International Trade in Endangered Species (CITES) and are listed under the agreement's Appendix II found at http://www.cites.org. This means that special permits are required for the import or export of these animals between countries. The related Indian python, *Python molurus molurus*, is considered endangered and listed as an Appendix I animal. It is also listed as endangered under the U.S. Endangered Species Act (ESA) and therefore requires special permits for transport between countries as well as for ownership and movement of animals between states within the United States.

For information on CITES and ESA permits and regulations, visit http://permits.fws.gov to find your region's contact information. This page will let you become familiar with the complications of any CITES or ESA permitting process. Also check their home page at http://www.fws.gov for an appreciation of the size of the Service.

Size

Hatchling Burmese pythons measure between 18 inches (runts) and 29 inches (46–74 cm). Breeders indicate an average length of 22 inches (56 cm) and an average weight of 4 ounces (113 grams) among captive-bred hatchlings. Female Burmese pythons can grow to lengths of 13 to 18 feet (4–5.4 m), and there are records of animals more than 19 feet (5.7 m) but no authenticated records of animals more than 20 feet (6 m). Males are typically smaller, their lengths ranging from 8 to 14 feet (2.4–4.2 m), though occasionally a male will grow to a length of 16 to 17 feet (4.8–5.1

m). For their size, Burmese pythons are among the heaviest of the giant snakes, with 17- to 18-foot (5.1–5.4 m) animals achieving weights of more than 200 pounds (90 kg).

Sexing

Hatchling Burmese pythons are easily sexed by manually everting the hemipenes in males so they project from their pouches behind the cloaca at the base of the tail. With this method, a hatchling python is held in such a way that the hind part of the body is positioned belly side up within the hand. The thumb should hold the area just in front of the vent (opening to the cloaca) against the index finger, and the base of the tail (just past the vent) rests on the index finger. With the thumb of the other hand, using a gentle rolling motion and starting at an area about a half inch (12 millimeters) past the vent, roll the thumb while applying pressure toward the vent. If done correctly, this will cause the hemipenes to evert in males. This method should only be performed by people experienced with the process. A snake can easily be injured by an inexperienced individual applying undue pressure to the area.

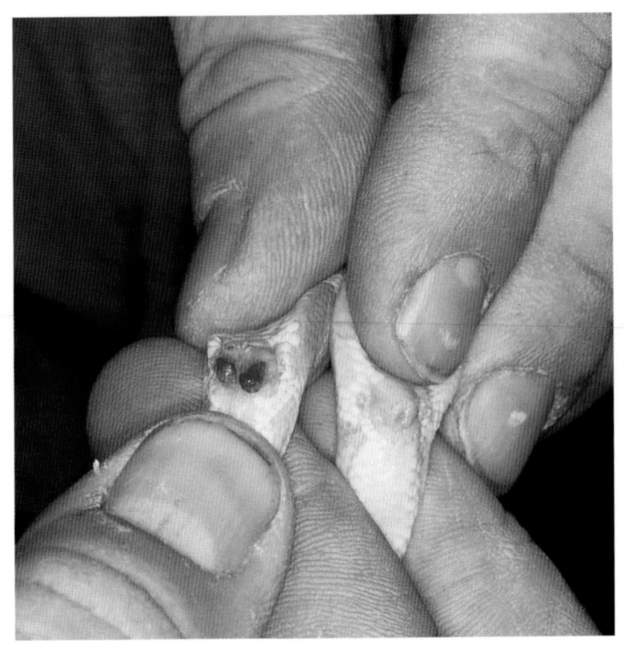

A professional shows how to manually sex two hatchling Burmese pythons. An everted hemipene shows the snake on the left is male; the absence of the hemipene on the snake at right indicates it's a female.

Lack of an everted hemipene indicates the specimen is either a female, or a male with very strong muscles at the hemipene bases. As a backup, hatchlings that appear to be females (no hemipene everted) can be probed with a 1-mm sexing probe. Females will probe to a depth of three to five subcaudal scales. Hatchling males will probe to a depth of eight or nine subcaudal scales; adult males will probe to a depth of ten to sixteen subcaudals.

Adults can only be reliably sexed through probing, though several characteristics can provide useful (but not always reliable) clues to the sex of animals. For example, females are usually of a larger size than males; males have larger spurs to the sides of the vent and have broader, thicker tails than females. Besides probing, breeding behaviors are very good indicators of sex.

Probing an adult Burmese python is a two-person operation. One individual will have to control the snake being probed and firmly hold and present, belly side up, the vent area of the snake toward the individual performing the probing. One method that will help control large snakes and facilitate probing is to put the snake in a cloth snake bag, allowing only the tail to remain outside. For Burmese pythons, 2-mm probes will work well depending on size.

To probe a Burmese python, the area just in front of the vent should be held with one hand and the thumb used to pull back the area in front (remember: "in front" means toward the head) of the anal scale to expose the cloacal opening. After moistening the probe with clean water, use the other hand to gently insert the probe, with a slight twirling motion, into one of the two small openings visible to the sides of the cloacal opening. In adult females, the probe will enter a musk gland to a length of three to five subcaudal scales, while in adult males it will enter an inverted hemipenis to a length of ten to sixteen subcaudal scales. To verify a reading, the process can be repeated on the other side. This is a procedure that is best performed and taught by experienced individuals. Most specialized reptile dealers will perform this service when you intend to buy animals of specific sexes.

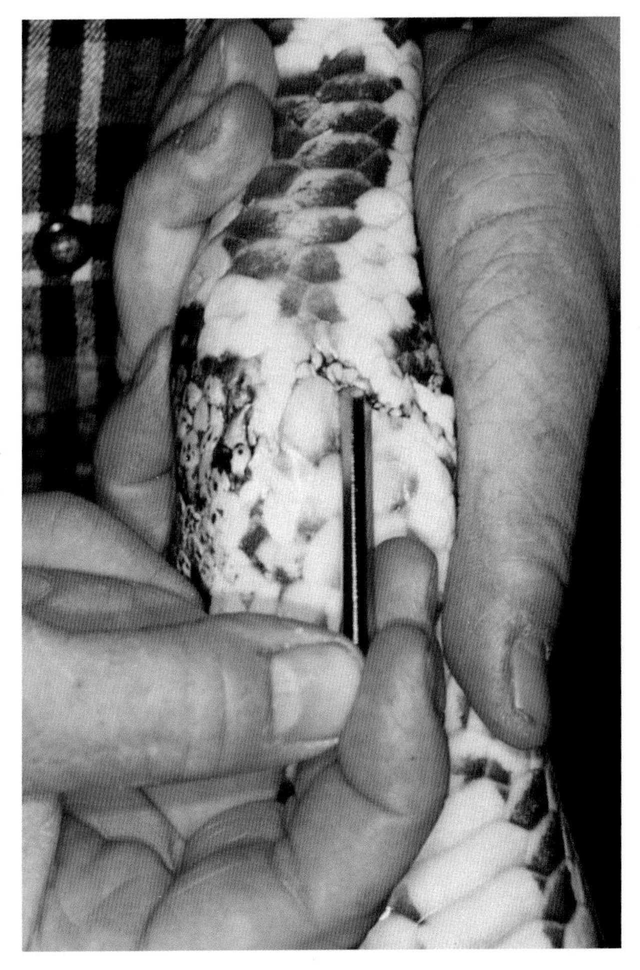

A sexing probe will reach a depth of three to five subcaudal scales in females and ten to sixteen subcaudal scales in males.

Ontogeny

This term refers to the stages of development an animal undergoes between birth and death. Any good animal person is aware of these stages and adjusts their husbandry to accommodate related requirements. With large pythons most of these husbandry adjustments involve feeding and temperature regimens. The following is a rough model of ontogeny as applied to Burmese pythons. Because environmental conditions and feeding regimens play such important roles in the rate of growth and maturation, the proposed duration of stages is tentative.

- Stage 1: Embryonic. This stage follows fertilization of an ovum and is spent within the confines of the egg. Egg and hatchling size and health will depend on the genetics of the parents, their health including fat reserves, and incubation parameters such as temperature and relative humidity.
- Stage 2: Juvenile to subadult. This stage begins at hatching and extends for fifteen to thirty-six months or more. It is characterized by a rapid growth rate from about 4 ounces (112 g) to around 30 pounds (13.5 kg) for females. Hatchlings may initially demonstrate a defensive behavior that consists of striking toward large

This Burmese python is only two days old.

moving objects (e.g., a human), but most will quickly habituate and relax. This stage is presexual and has a high potential for rapid growth. Intense feeding regimens (called *power feeding* by some) combined with temperatures in the upper 80s F can lead Burmese pythons to become sexually mature by eighteen months or about 10 feet (3 m) long for females, which will end this stage. Under less intensive feeding regimens females may take three years or more to become sexually mature.
- Stage 3: Young adult (sexual onset). This stage is triggered by an increase in sex hormones leading to physiological and behavioral changes, including courtship and

copulatory behaviors in males; and receptivity, ova maturation, and ovulation in females. As a rule, young adult snakes are the best breeders because their smaller size allows them to regain the weight loss from breeding relatively quickly. Note that most accidents and deaths involving Burmese pythons seem to have been caused by late Stage 2 to early Stage 3 animals in the 8 feet to 11 feet (2.4–3.3 m) range. With Stage 3 animals, the relative growth compared to the juvenile stage slows but it is still significant. This stage lasts several years. Female pythons will steadily grow during Stage 3, potentially increasing their sexual onset weight many times until they reach a size where additional growth is minimal. Herpetoculturists interested in breeding Burmese pythons adjust the feeding and temperature regimens of Stage 3 animals as mentioned under the Prebreeding Conditioning section in the Breeding chapter.

- Stage 4: Maturity. This stage is characterized by either insignificant (males) or greatly reduced (females) growth rates. In short, growth seems to stabilize. Under optimal conditions, this leveling off occurs at four to five years past sexual onset. At this stage, female Burmese pythons are large snakes, relatively slow moving and often very energy conservative. They will fare well on one meal every ten days and can survive for years on just one large meal a month offered for six or seven months out of the year. Stage 4 females often will not breed annually and regularly skip years. Herpetoculturists must make efforts not to overfeed Stage 4 animals so as to prevent obesity. These large pythons are not ideal if the primary goal is high-production captive breeding.
- Stage 5: Old age. Many reptiles, even snakes, eventually show signs of old age characterized by little to no growth, reduced feeding, reduced shedding rates, and often, in the case of females, reduced breeding frequency or cessation of breeding. This stage ends with death.

Growth

Under captive conditions, Burmese pythons will grow to sexual maturity at an amazing rate. Growth rates achieved by herpetoculturists with females under optimal feeing conditions typically show the following growth pattern:

- By the end of twelve months, expect growth to a length of 6 to 9 feet (1.8–2.9 m).
- By eighteen months, expect growth to between 9 and 10 feet (2.7–3.2 m). Breeding is initiated soon after this time, and the growth rate from there on slows down considerably.
- Breeders record growth rates of 12 to 18 inches (30.5–45.7 cm) a year for the first two to three years following the 10-foot mark (3-m) and, thus, first breeding. Thereafter, the growth rate will continue to decline with age, though there are reports of older animals entering a period of accelerated growth following several years of typically reduced growth. There can be a wide range of variation in the growth and length of captive-raised specimens depending on genetic background, feeding, and breeding regimens.

Burmese Python Morphs

A number of Burmese python morphs have been established and are now regularly captive-bred and offered in the pet trade. The recent discovery of a dwarf morph will likely result in future dwarf versions of all the current morphs. The following is an overview of the most commonly offered varieties of Burmese pythons.

- Albino: This is a simple recessive trait. Typical albino Burmese are yellow, white, and orange. The albino trait can be combined with any other morph, such as albino patternless and albino labyrinth Burmese pythons.
- Patternless or green: This is a simple recessive trait that results in a nearly patternless adult snake that is mostly uniform faded brown to dark or khaki green. Juveniles have some pattern remnants that mostly fade as the snake matures.
- Labyrinth: This is another simple recessive trait charac-

Albino Burmese can be yellow, orange, or white as shown here.

terized by a variable broken maze-like pattern and striping on the first quarter of the body.

- Granite: This simple recessive trait is characterized by an intricate fine, broken, almost peppered pattern. The heads of granite Burmese have an even, light tan color with a faded brown middorsal spear pattern.
- Dwarf: The dream of many to own a snake with the calm demeanor and docile temperament of a Burmese python that remains at a safe and manageable size may soon be realized. A dwarf Burmese python has become available. Dwarf Burmese pythons hatch out at a fraction of the size of typical Burmese pythons, weighing only 1.9 to 2.3 ounces (54–67 g) versus the 4 ounces

This green Burmese has nearly patternless skin, a common trait among adult snakes of this morph. Juvenile green morphs may display slight markings, which should fade as they mature.

This snake displays the peppered markings along its body and a faded pattern on its head that is typical with granite morphs.

plus (112+ g) of standard hatchlings. Females become sexually mature by 5 feet and 7 pounds (1.5 m, 3.2 kg). Few dwarf Burmese pythons are currently in captivity, but breeders are steadily working to make this desirable morph more readily available.

CHAPTER 2

SELECTION

Initial selection of a Burmese python is a critical first step that will determine the probability of your success at raising the animal to maturity as well as the long-term relationship you will have with the animal. The following are guidelines that should help you select a potentially healthy Burmese python as well as one which will be likely to become a good pet with a docile personality.

Captive-Bred Versus Wild-Caught

The first choice when contemplating the purchase of a Burmese python should be a captive-bred hatchling from a reliable breeder. Captive-bred Burmese pythons are less likely to harbor diseases than are imported snakes.

As a second choice, imported hatchling Burmese are the next best selection. As a precaution, it is recommended that you have the stools (feces) of any imported Burmese checked for internal parasites including protozoans such as *Entamoeba* and *Trichomonas*. It is also a good idea to have them checked for salmonellosis.

Selecting a Potentially Healthy Snake

Whether you are buying a captive-bred or an imported Burmese python, careful attention should be given to the selection of an animal to determine visually and through handling the probability of its being healthy and docile.

The following are guidelines for selection to help you determine the health status of the snake:

- Prior to requesting that a specific snake be handed over to you for inspection, select snakes that have rounded bodies and that don't demonstrate pronounced backbone or rib definition. Check that the skin is relatively clear and free of superficial injuries. Avoid runts.

This Burmese python is underweight, dehydrated, and affected by a chronic respiratory disease. Burmese disease is the primary consideration, although inclusion body disease (IBD) should also be investigated.

- Ask that the python be handed over to you. Once in hand, a healthy Burmese python should give a distinct impression of strength and good muscle tone. Avoid snakes that give an impression of limpness and poor muscle tone. The latter are always reliable indicators of poor health.
- Hold the snake behind its head with one hand and, using the other hand, gently pull down the skin underneath the lower jaw to open its mouth. Look for bubbly mucus which is a sign of a respiratory infection.

  Another technique (though not as reliable) to determine this is to leave the mouth of the snake closed and, using the thumb of your free hand, gently press up against the throat area. This often will cause mucus to emerge from the sides of the mouth or the nostrils in snakes with respiratory infections. Avoid snakes with these symptoms.
- Repeating the aforementioned procedure for opening the snake's mouth, look for signs of mouth rot (stomatitis). This will appear as areas on the gums covered with caseous (cheesy-looking) matter. In some cases red, raw, and injured areas will be present. Again, avoid purchasing snakes with these symptoms.
- While in hand, check the eyes to make sure that they are clear. If the snake is in shed, both eyes should demonstrate equal levels of opacity (clouding over).

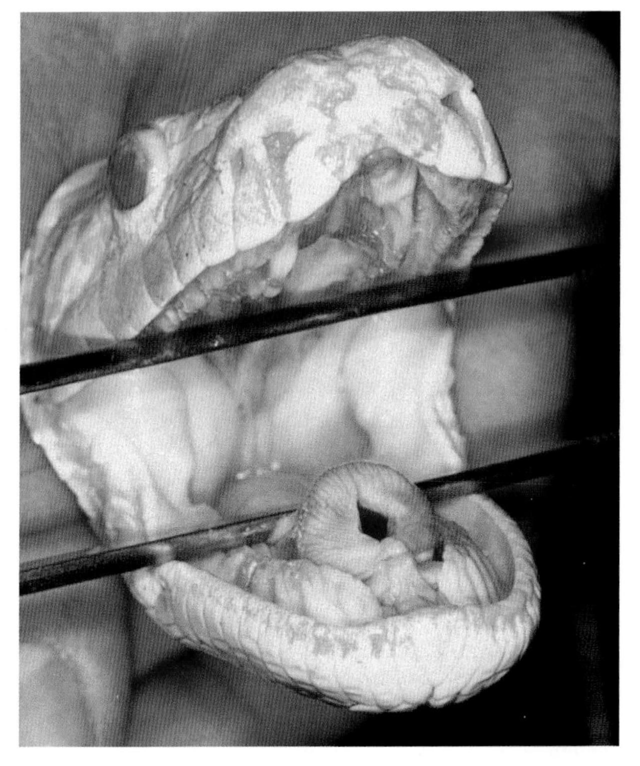

This healthy Burmese shows no signs of mouth rot. Bubbly mucus, cheese-like matter along the gums, and mouth sores are all indicators of disease or infection.

- Check the body for bumps and depressed areas along the backbone. Check for collapsed areas along the sides of the body; these are signs of broken ribs. Avoid snakes with any of these symptoms.
- Check the belly area to make sure that it is free of signs of skin infection (raised ventral scales, stained and damaged scales, etc.).
- Check the vent (opening to the cloaca) to make sure the anal scale lies flat against the body and is free of any caked or crusty matter. Make sure that the surrounding area is free of signs of smeared diarrhea. Avoid snakes with these symptoms.
- Look for mites. These tiny, round, bead-like arthropods, when present, can be seen moving on the body. They can also be seen imbedded between the rims of the eyes and on the eyes themselves, giving a raised impression to the rims. Two reliable indicators of mites

Select a Burmese with healthy skin like this snake's. Do not purchase a snake if you see mites crawling on the animal or on your hands after handling the snake. Do not risk infecting other snakes in your collection.

are the presence of scattered slivery white flecks (mite feces) on the body of a snake and, following inspection of a snake, the presence of tiny mites crawling on your hands. If you have other snakes in your collection, it is recommended to not purchase snakes with these parasites.

Docility

Hatchling Burmese may initially be nippy. However, specimens that will become very docile tend to settle down, stop biting, and move more calmly after some gentle handling. At the other extreme are young Burmese that try to get out of your hands as quickly as they can, defecate, and bite repeatedly when restrained. Other individuals demonstrate behaviors that range somewhere in between. If docility when handling is an important to you (as it should be), then pay extra attention to this area when selecting your Burmese python.

Temperament

No studies have been done to clearly determine the relationship of genetics to temperament in Burmese pythons. Many people have the notion that virtually any Burmese can become tame with handling, but that is simply not true. In the opinion and experience of the author and other herpetoculturists, genetics plays a crucial role in the determination of "personality" in Burmese pythons. These differences in temperament often are obvious even when the animals are young. Some Burmese are simply nasty, and even with regular handling they will remain nervous and likely to bite. Some have calm dispositions that are apparent early on and persist as the snakes mature. Others are somewhere in between, not really nasty but not calm either; they remain nervous when handled though they may be reluctant to bite.

The author suspects that these traits of temperament are genetically determined and that selective breeding for good temperament by herpetoculturists is desirable if Burmese pythons are to become more widespread as reptile pets. With Burmese pythons, initial temperament plays a key role to subsequent human behavior rather than the other way around (human behavior influencing temperament). As a rule, the more docile a Burmese python is to start with, the more frequently it will be handled. On the other hand, the reverse is true: a nasty Burmese gets handled less frequently because its owner eventually dreads the chore of having to deal with it. With Burmese pythons, personality should be at least as important as looks. How about 14 feet (4.2 m) of nasty good looks to deal with on a weekly basis?

CHAPTER 3

HOUSING AND MAINTENANCE

Only the smallest Burmese pythons can be housed in all-glass enclosures with screen tops, and you might as well plan from the beginning on a well-built cage suitable for holding a very large, heavy snake. Makeshift cages just won't work.

Enclosures

Enclosure Location

It is important that enclosures be placed in spacious rooms to facilitate maintenance and handling. An adult Burmese python in a cluttered room can readily topple furniture in the course of handling. From a safety point of view, a cluttered room will not allow you the maneuverability recommended to safely and responsibly maintain and handle these pythons. It is recommended that any room where Burmese pythons are maintained be kept locked when the owners are not present. This will prevent possible tampering by children or guests. If you inspect and repair holes in the wall and other openings and methodically shut windows when leaving the room, a locked room will contain a snake in case of an escape. Escapes will not occur if you are a responsible herpetoculturist and have an appropriate enclosure with a locking mechanism.

Security

Enclosures for Burmese pythons should be specifically designed for housing large snakes. They should have either a

This reticulated python injured its face and mouth from repeated rubbing against its cage screen. Enclosures must have proper locking mechanisms to prevent escapes by curious snakes exploring their cages.

sliding or hinged cover or sliding or hinged front (either clear Plexiglas panels, framed Plexiglas or quarter-inch (6-mm) tempered glass doors) with a locking mechanism that prevents any risk of accidental escape by the snake. Such locking mechanisms will vary depending on the enclosure design. Virtually all escapee large constrictors result from inadequate housing at home or during transport. A common stupid practice for covering the cages of large snakes is to place boards on top with rocks or books to keep the cover down. This method doesn't work and is irresponsible. If you can't build or buy an adequate cage, then you shouldn't own the snake.

At the time of writing, several companies offer either molded plastic or fiberglass enclosures with sliding glass fronts, such as the Vision Herpetological line, or melamine-covered wooden cages with hinged or sliding glass fronts large enough for housing Burmese pythons or other giant snakes. You can also have enclosures custom-built by companies that specialize in snake caging. If you are a decent carpenter and have the necessary tools, you can even build your own cage(s).

Enclosure Size

Juvenile giant snakes can all be started in relatively small cages, which will also make them feel secure. Hatchlings can be housed in 20- to 30-inch-long (51–76 cm) snake enclo-

This 75-gallon (284-liter) enclosure is suitable for a 6–8 foot (1.8–2.4 meter) Burmese.

sures and graduated to larger ones as they grow, estimating that the perimeter of an enclosure should be at least one and a half times the length of the snake. For adult female Burmese pythons or reticulated pythons, this means enclosures at least 72 x 36 inches (183 x 91 cm) and up to 96 inches (244 cm) long for unusually large specimens. Another option is to frame part of a room to create an insulated glass-fronted display, much as one sees in zoos.

Substrates

To make a fancy, attractive setup for a Burmese would require no less than a room-sized enclosure. Because of this, virtually all herpetoculturists choose to keep Burmese pythons under simple, easily maintained conditions. Using plants for decoration is virtually out of the question unless you have enough room to plant some large trees or shrubs and provide proper lighting for them (very unlikely). Select a substrate that is easily replaced such as aspen shavings, pine shavings, newspaper, rabbit pellets (compressed alfalfa), or fine orchid bark. The latter looks the most natural but should be thoroughly rinsed to remove any bark dust if you wish to have a clean-looking Burmese. If you have any notions of using anything fancy, just remember that when a big Burmese defecates it produces copious amounts of semi-solid and liquid matter. This is not necessarily a big deal in a room-sized enclosure, but in a relatively small enclosure the visual and olfactory impacts increase considerably. Simple, quick, and easy to clean are the best qualities of a good substrate and cage design.

Dry landscape materials can be used for decoration as long as they can be easily cleaned or removed. These can include large rocks, large select pieces of wood, large sections of cork bark, and dried grasses. For many reasons, including ease of handling, any decorations should be simple, leaving the cage uncluttered.

Temperature

Burmese pythons should be maintained at a temperature of 85–90 degrees F (29.5°C–32 °C), but the issue of providing adequate heat is not so simple. The best system is to provide a daytime air temperature of 84°F–88°F (29°C–31°C) with a heated basking area achieving a surface temperature of 88°F–92°F (31°C–33°C). By providing a heated area, you allow a Burmese python the opportunity to self-regulate its body temperature. At night, the air temperature can be allowed to drop to 80°F–84°F (26.5°C–29°C). In emergency situations, the nighttime temperature can safely be allowed to drop to 65°F (18°C) for brief periods of time (at most several hours). As long as a basking area is available, many of the problems associated with temperatures that are too cool (respiratory infections, inability to effectively digest food, increased susceptibility to disease) can be avoided.

During prebreeding conditioning, Burmese pythons will have to be maintained at cooler temperatures for several weeks (see chapter on Breeding).

Thermometers

Many herpetoculturists tend to play guessing games where temperature is concerned. They guesstimate the temperature of their rooms, of their setups, and of the basking areas.

Thermometers are useful tools that should be used by all herpetoculturists. Currently several types of thermometers are available. They range from the standard glass-bulb mercury thermometers (now generally using mercury substitutes) to stick-on thermographic (liquid crystal) thermometers, which some companies now sell as wide-range thermometers for use with reptiles, to electronic thermometers.

The author's favorite and most recommended thermometers for keeping reptiles are electronic thermometers with sensors and an alarm that will warn you when the measured temperature is outside of the range that you set. These thermometers are sold in electronic supply stores for $20 to $35 (depending on their features) at the time of writing. At one setting you can get a continuous visual readout of the room temperature. By switching the setting, you can also get a visual readout of the temperature through a remote sensing probe (which can be placed in the basking area or inside an incubator) connected to the thermometer. At the push of a button, some of these thermometers will also give you the minimum/maximum reading over twenty-four hours. Modern electronic thermometers are invaluable to herpetoculturists and should be used more widely.

Heating Systems

Giant snakes should be given the opportunity to thermoregulate by having a section, about a third of the cage surface, heated to 88°F–90°F (31°C–32°C), except when conditioning for breeding (see the Prebreeding Conditioning section in the Breeding chapter). Note that a common cause of death with large snakes is respiratory infections incurred during the winter when they are kept too cool, usually because the heating unit is too small or inadequate.

Heat Pads and Heat Tapes

The easiest method to heat enclosures is to use either a sub-tank heating unit such as a reptile heating pad or wide heat tape (e.g., Flexwatt) connected to a thermostat with a temperature probe. These are now sold through specialized reptile stores and mail-order reptile supply companies.

Pig Blankets (Plastic-Enclosed Heating Pads)

You may have never heard of these, but they are the best commercially produced heating units for large reptiles. They are sold or can be special-ordered through feed stores. Pig blankets are large—usually at least 3 feet x 1 foot (76 x 30 cm)—rigid plastic-enclosed units that provide a high surface heat over a broad area. For use with large reptiles, these units must be controlled with an appropriate thermostat that can be special-ordered from the manufacturer.

Ceramic Heat Emitters

As a source of overhead heat, ceramic heat emitters now sold in the reptile trade are an efficient way to warm an enclosure without the bright light of incandescent bulbs. Make sure you select the right wattage bulb for the size of the enclosure and use a ceramic base fixture capable of handling the wattage (plastic sockets with cardboard liners will burn after a few hours). Always place the bulb over one end of an enclosure so the snake has a cool area to which it can retire. The heat output of ceramic emitters can be controlled with rheostats or thermostats.

Incandescent Lights

Incandescent bulbs, spotlights, or floodlights in an appropriate fixture (generally an aluminum cone or hemisphere called a clamplight) can also be used to keep pythons warm. The important point is to measure the temperature at the basking area immediately underneath the fixture and at the distance furthest from the bulb after the bulb has been on for at least an hour. A 100-watt bulb in a metal clamplight can produce high temperatures if too close to the basking area. Incandescent bulbs must always be outside the enclosure where they cannot burn the snake.

Space Heaters and Room Heaters

These heaters, easily obtainable from most department and hardware stores, are frequently used by herpetoculturists maintaining large collections in special snake rooms. All things considered, they are one of the best and most economical systems for heating a room, but they do have problems. Virtually all of the problems have to do with the risk of overheating. Every year there is at least one story of an individual losing their entire collection because the thermostat failed and the unit kept running. A recent incident involved a python breeder who lost virtually every Burmese python in his possession including albino Burmese. The lesson here is that a system has to be devised to prevent overheating. Either purchase a thermostat or set up an alarm that will warn you when the temperature goes over (or under) a set temperature.

Aside from thermostats failing, one cause of heaters failing to perform satisfactorily involves placement. If you place a heater on the floor where there is a cool draft, the thermostat on the heater senses the floor's cooler temperature instead of the room temperature, causing the heater to continue running. Also remember that a room heater will create heat gradients, with temperatures near the ceiling as much as ten degrees F (about five degrees C) higher than temperatures near the ground. One practice that can help reduce the incidence of thermostat failure is to replace heaters on a regular basis. Some keepers will do it every year as standard practice. Thermostats are more likely to fail on old heaters.

Take notice of the above warning and buy thermometers and thermostats and do what you have to do. Don't procrastinate—this is serious stuff. Heed this warning!

Fire Prevention

Read instructions carefully regarding heater use and be careful and responsible in terms of placement.

Hot Rocks

As a rule, "hot rock" type heaters can present problems for snakes. However, at least some brands of hot rocks if used properly can be used when raising hatchling pythons. The key is to measure surface temperature, which should be 85°F–95°F (29.5°C–35°C). If the surface temperature exceeds 95°F (35°C), place a thin, flat rock on top to diffuse the surface heat and measure the temperature again. If it is within the appropriate range, this system will be suitable for raising hatchling and juvenile Burmese. Eventually the snake

A space heater is an economical option for heating your enclosure, but the unit's thermostat is not fail-proof. Also be aware that a heater placed on the floor in a draft may cause the unit to sense the floor's cooler temperature rather than the enclosure's interior temperature. Replace old heaters and thermometers to reduce the possibility of overheating your snake.

will outgrow any size hot rock you might purchase and you will have to resort to other heating systems.

Precautions

Extreme care must be given to assure that light and heating fixtures and bulbs are placed outside of the cage with screening to prevent any possible direct contact with the bulb. Snakes are not normally exposed to searing heat in the wild, and they tend to be stupid in terms of judging their tolerance to hot surfaces. Thermal burns caused by poorly placed and poorly protected light fixtures are a common veterinary problem with captive reptiles. So think snake and keep that bulb away. Also be sure to place the fixture in such a way that no object, cloth, etc., is likely to make contact with the bulb or unit outside the enclosure. Think fire prevention.

Some herpetoculturists, after carefully determining the position of the heating elements within the fiberglass, will bolt one of these units on a piece of plywood raised above 12-inch (30-cm) legs to create a heated platform. When keeping more than one python in a large cage, this platform will provide a heated area for a python lying on top as well as provide overhead heating for the animal using the underside as a shelter. Before making any such modifications for your personal use, read instructions carefully and if necessary contact the manufacturing company for any additional information as to proper use. For keeping large pythons warm, there is nothing like them.

Maintenance

A weekly maintenance schedule should be implemented with Burmese pythons. Clean the enclosure to remove feces and replace areas of soiled substrate as needed. The water container should be cleaned and disinfected and the water replaced at least on a weekly basis. Know where the snake is at all times or relocate it to a temporary container during cleaning. Always have an assistant present when dealing with large snakes.

Tools

Many herpetoculturists resort to several tools for maintaining their Burmese pythons. One of the most widely used tools for handling large snakes is a snake stick or hook, which can be purchased from a specialized dealer. Tongs or large tweezers are useful when feeding Burmese. Other tools used to maintain Burmese pythons include various "shields" that are custom-made by herpetoculturists to suit their purposes. A shield usually consists of a section of Plexiglas or plywood with a handle attached to its center. Some herpetoculturists also put a 4-inch (10-cm) lip around the shield. Others use both small and large shields. A Plexiglas shield or a wooden shield with a section of Plexiglas in the center have the advantage of providing visibility. Typical uses of shields are to create a barrier between oneself and a snake when removing food or cleaning litter. Large shields with a wide lip can be placed over a coiled Burmese while cleaning the cage or when removing the eggs. The need to use tools will vary depending on the setup, the nature and number of animals being worked, and the maintenance routines established.

CHAPTER 4

FEEDING

Following hatching, Burmese pythons will begin to feed soon after their first shed. As a rule, Burmese pythons feed readily at all sizes and present no problems in this area. The best and most readily available foods for Burmese pythons are commercially bred rodents starting with mice for hatchlings, then rats of an appropriate size, and eventually rabbits. Most Burmese pythons will readily feed on both live and prekilled rodents to prevent any possible injury to the snake and to minimize suffering in the prey animal.

Prey Size Guidelines

As a rule, width of a prey item should not be greater than the greatest apparent width measured at midbody of the snake. It is important to feed prey items of the appropriate size. Prey items that are too large may be eaten but run a high risk of being regurgitated at a later time.

Thus, hatchlings should initially be fed just-weaned mice. After a few feedings, you can offer adult mice. If you

A young adult or juvenile Burmese at least 4 feet long can usually be fed small rats; gradually increase the size of the prey as the snake grows.

offer prey of adequate size, you can start by feeding your snake one prey item and then introducing a second prey item. If your Burmese python is still hungry, it may feed on the second prey item; if not, it will usually leave it alone. By the time they are 4 feet (1.2 m) long, Burmese pythons should be fed small rats and should gradually be offered bigger rats as they become larger. By the time they reach 6 to 7 feet (1.8–2.1 m), they can be switched from large rats to small rabbits. As they grow older, Burmese should gradually be fed larger rabbits.

Live Versus Prekilled Prey

Burmese can be fed prekilled prey from the time they are hatchlings. The advantage to feeding prekilled prey is that it minimizes suffering in the prey animal and it minimizes the possibility of bite damage to a pet python. It also makes offering and removing a prey animal easier. One method of humanely killing mice and rats is to grab one by the tail and, with a swift motion, strike the back of the head against the edge of a table. With rabbits, the best method is to ask your supplier to kill them at the time of purchase.

It is recommended that all prey animals be offered live or prekilled soon after removal from their rearing cages. It has been suggested that vitamin C and other nutrients from food remaining in the prey animal's gut contents may be beneficial to snakes. For example, vitamin C has been shown to play a role in reducing the probability of stomatitis (mouth rot) and in maintaining the integrity of the skin. As with all predators, when a snake ingests its prey, it also ingests the gut contents of the prey. Thus, care should be given to assure that prey animals are fed a high-quality diet.

Other Foods

Some herpetoculturists occasionally feed their Burmese prekilled whole chickens. The fact is that Burmese pythons, like many other larger snakes, like fowl of any type. In Southeast Asia, Burmese pythons kept as pets or on display are often maintained on a diet consisting primarily of fowl (captive-bred rats and rabbits are not readily available in

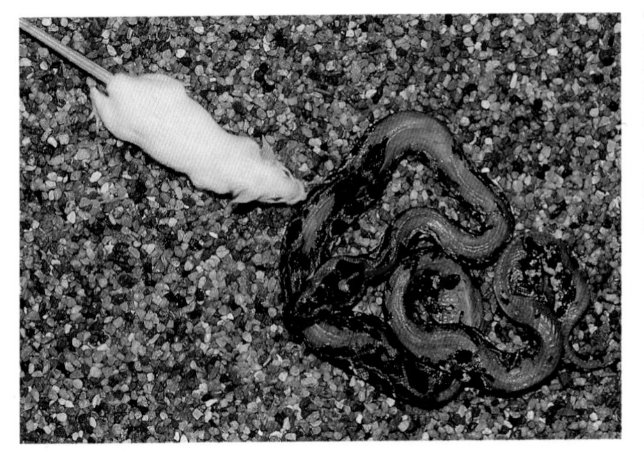

Feeding live prey introduces the possibility of injury to your snake as shown here with a Burmese python that was bitten multiple times by the rat.

Asian countries). Burmese pythons that for one reason or another are off feed will often feed with great enthusiasm on chickens, and most Burmese will readily feed on raw chicken parts such as chicken thighs or drumsticks from the market.

However, caution should be used when feeding fowl in any form. A significant percentage of raw chicken parts sold in markets will test positive for *Salmonella*. If feeding live or prekilled chickens, care must be given to the selection of the source. The best would be to raise chickens at home under relatively hygienic conditions. Many herpetoculturists prekill all fowl and freeze them for several weeks prior to feeding.

As a rule, fowl should only be used as a last resort for fattening Burmese pythons that are reluctant to feed, such as an import or to put on that extra bit of weight right before prebreeding conditioning.

Feeding Regimens

The growth of your Burmese python will be directly related to its feeding regimen (all other conditions being adequate, such as temperature). The growth rate of Burmese pythons is greatest during the first eighteen months to three years, at which point they reach sexual maturity and thereafter slow down considerably, though Burmese pythons can and will grow for most of their lives.

The feeding regimen of a Burmese python should be adjusted to its growth rate and overall appearance and condition. A standard procedure involves optimal feeding (power feeding) for the first two to three years, cutting down on the regimen when growth rate slows down to prevent the risk of obesity. Adjustments are also made with breeding females to optimize breeding condition. For good breeding results, females, as a rule, should have good weight but should not be obese. Following egg-laying, females are often fed more frequently to make up for weight loss. These are all factors that must be taken into account when determining feeding regimens.

- From hatchling to 4 feet (1.2 m): Feed one or two mice of an appropriate size every three to four days.
- From 4 feet (1.2 m) to sexual maturity (usually around 10 feet [3 m] in females and around 8 feet [2.4 m] in males): Feed one or two prey animals every five to seven days.
- At 4 feet (1.2 m): Switch to medium rats, then slowly graduate to larger rats. By 6 to 7 feet (1.8–2.1 m), switch to 3-pound (1.4-kg) rabbits. Increase the size of the rabbit(s) as the snake grows.
- From sexual maturity (approximately eighteen months) to three years: Feed one or two rabbits once a week.
- From three years on: Feed one or two rabbits every ten days, with adjustments depending on overall appearance of the snake. Snakes that are bred every year and allowed to brood eggs may have to be fed every week to regain enough weight in six months to be able to breed the following year. Use your judgment.

Stunting

Burmese pythons that are fed infrequently or offered small amounts of food per feeding during the first twelve to eighteen months of life will be seriously stunted and may require several years to achieve a size suitable for breeding. These animals often remain stunted for life, never achieving a normal size for the species. Some of these animals during the course of such a starvation program will also tend to become aggressive (who can blame them?).

The Right Way to Feed Burmese Pythons

Up to a length of 6 feet (1.8 m), Burmese pythons can be fed without special precautions other than being careful when placing food into the cage or removing it. Once they reach a length greater than 6 feet (1.8 m), it is critical that a herpetoculturist adopt safe feeding procedures to prevent the possibility of injury to oneself. The following are sound feeding procedures:

- Only house one snake per cage and thus feed only one snake per cage at a time.
- Have prey items within reach. Determine where the snake is before opening the door—the snake should be away from the door. If it is near the door, open the door and move the snake away with a snake stick. Then toss the prey item from a distance onto a suitable site in the cage or introduce the prey item using a long pair of snake tongs. Under no circumstance should you hold a prey item by the tail or scruff of the neck to offer it to the snake until it grabs it out of your hand. Don't be stupid.
- If the snake doesn't feed and you have to remove the prey, open the cage and use a snake stick to push the snake away from the vicinity of the prey; then push the prey item toward the door. Remove the prey with a large set of tongs; remove the prey with your hand only if the snake is at the other end of a large cage and well out of possible striking range of your hand or the prey item you are grabbing. A safe method is to place a small wooden board or a shield between the snake and yourself prior to removing any prey item.

Water

Burmese pythons in the wild are often found near water. In captivity, water should regularly be made available in a large, sturdy water bowl or, if one can afford the space, in a small pool. Aside from the necessity of providing water, a water container will also raise the air humidity in the vivarium and will provide an area for soaking that will facilitate proper shedding of the skin.

A problem when using large pools involves cleaning, since Burmese pythons will frequently defecate in a container of water. All efforts should be made to provide water in a container that can be regularly cleaned and disinfected in a 5 percent chlorine solution (unscented bleach from the supermarket). Containers that are allowed to remain foul will encourage the growth of microorganisms that can lead to disease. It is best to establish maintenance procedures and routines that allow for regularly providing clean water in clean containers.

CHAPTER 5

BREEDING

Burmese pythons are among the easiest to breed of all snakes. They can reach sexual maturity by eighteen months of age and have relatively high reproductive rates.

Prebreeding Factors

Prior to breeding Burmese pythons, you should make sure that you have properly sexed pairs, that they are of a size that makes it highly probable that they are sexually mature, and that any snakes selected for breeding are disease-free and have adequate weight. It is generally recommended that female Burmese pythons be slightly overweight prior to breeding. Underweight, obviously thin females should not be bred. Minimum recommended breeding size for female Burmese pythons is 9 feet (2.85 m), but larger is preferable. Males should be at least 8 feet (2.4 m) though some males are sexually mature at 7 feet (2.1 m).

Breeding Age

Burmese pythons (if captive-raised and optimally fed) will be sexually mature by eighteen months of age, but some breeders who are not as eager to breed their snakes as quickly as possible prefer waiting an extra year or two before mating their female Burmese pythons. The result is being able to keep female Burmese on a nearly year-round feeding schedule for that extra one or two years. Within that period of time these females can achieve an extra foot (30 cm) or more in length compared to early-bred Burmese, which once they begin breeding will be off feed four to six months out of a year. Some breeders claim that the benefits of delaying breeding are larger females that, once they begin breeding, will consistently produce larger clutches compared to early-bred Burmese pythons.

Following a hatchling's first shed, a young Burmese will be ready to feed on just-weaned mice.

On the other hand, some of the top Burmese python breeders in the United States claim that in the long run there is no significant difference in reproductive performance between early-bred and later-bred Burmese pythons. To a great degree, the maintenance schedule and the consequent size and weight of Burmese pythons (particularly females) should be the determining factors as to whether they are ready to breed.

Breeding Profiles

Optimal breeding frequency in Burmese pythons tends to occur within the first few years following sexual maturity. As the snakes get larger and older, some may not necessarily breed every year but will occasionally skip a year and eventually may skip more than a year between breedings. The fact is that there is variation in Burmese pythons in terms of their breeding potential. Some females will breed every year for ten years in a row, while others will routinely skip years. Some females, as they become older, may stop breeding altogether. Though older snakes may breed less frequently than younger animals, they often make up for it by producing larger numbers of eggs. Not enough data are available to present a long-term profile of intensive captive breeding of Burmese pythons. In time, enough information will be available to determine optimal breeding schedules, breeding age, and the point where Burmese may become past their prime and past optimal economic returns.

Prebreeding Conditioning

Prior to breeding, Burmese pythons should be exposed to a cool rest period for four to eight weeks. During that time, the basking and heating units are turned off and the enclosure temperature determined exclusively by air temperature. Many herpetoculturists cool their Burmese pythons on a schedule beginning any time between October 15 and January 1 by allowing the temperature in their cages to drop to a minimum of 65°F (18°C) (the mid 70s F is the most desirable) at night, with maximum daytime temperatures in the lower 80s F. Some breeders also use a method whereby the room temperature (and thus air temperature in the enclosure) is maintained at a temperature of 75°F–78°F (24°C–25.5°C) around the clock during the cooling period. During that time the snakes are carefully monitored to assure that they do not develop respiratory infections.

This prebreeding conditioning is essential for consistent and controlled breeding of Burmese pythons. During this period, the Burmese pythons are not fed. The cooling is believed to alter the metabolic pathways in females such that they ovulate following cooling and stored fat is converted to maturing eggs. In males, cooling is believed to lead to an increase in male hormones, increasing fertility through the production of healthy and active sperm.

Breeding

Following the prebreeding conditioning, the temperature is returned to normal and female snakes are placed back on a high-frequency feeding schedule (food offered every five days). Male Burmese pythons will typically fast following cooling and through the actual breeding period. Starting about three weeks after returning to a normal schedule, the female is introduced into a male's cage. Some herpetoculturists at this point keep pairs together, while others remove and reintroduce pairs, allowing them to spend a couple of days together once or twice a week. By introducing or pairing a female alternately with more than one male, chances of high fertility will be increased. Copulation once initiated will last for several hours. Once mating activity begins, females will usually stop feeding.

An alternative method to induce breeding used by some breeders is to keep the snakes at a temperature of 75°F–78°F (24°C–25.5°C) during the prebreeding conditioning and during breeding for a total period of eight to ten weeks. With this method, females are not put back on a standard feeding schedule and the snakes are introduced or kept in pairs beginning with the fourth week following the initiation of cooling. By the end of the eight- to ten-week cooling period, females will usually be gravid.

Gravid females will continue to fast during the entire period of egg development and, if allowed to incubate their eggs, will continue to fast up to the time of hatching, a total fasting period that can last up to six months. If you incubate the eggs artificially, females can be induced to resume feeding by moving them regularly away from a spot where they may initiate brooding behavior. Many females will persist brooding for varying periods of time even though their eggs have been removed.

Egg-laying will usually occur two to three months following the observation of copulations. Many breeders provide a shallow nest box with barely moist sphagnum moss as an egg-laying site (see Maternal Incubation section following). The female will undergo a shed two to four weeks (most herpetoculturists report four weeks to thirty days) prior to egg-laying. Depending on their prebreeding conditioning and breeding schedules, breeders have reported females laying eggs between January and July, but most eggs of Burmese pythons in captivity are laid between February and June.

Clutch Size

Depending on the snake's size, weight, and other factors, the number of eggs laid by a female Burmese python will vary. As a rule, the larger the female, the more eggs she will lay. At a size of 9 to 10 feet (2.9 to 3.2 m) when first breeding may be initiated, females will typically lay from eighteen to twenty-five eggs, but there are reports of forty-two to forty-

This two-day-old hatchling Burmese is still with the remaining eggs from its clutch.

five eggs being laid by females bred at an age of eighteen months. During the second year of breeding, egg clutches will typically range from twenty-five to thirty-eight eggs, with many reports of significantly larger clutches. As females grow larger, more eggs are usually produced (also dependent on the overall condition including fat reserves). There is a record of a large female Burmese python laying a clutch of 107 eggs.

Incubation

There are two widely used methods for incubating the eggs of Burmese and other pythons: maternal and artificial incubation.

Maternal Incubation

A method increasingly used by herpetoculturists is to allow the females to incubate their eggs. To do this, a nest box consisting of a wooden frame 2 feet x 2 feet and 6 inches tall (61 x 61 cm, 15 cm tall) is placed inside the female's enclosure. Within two weeks following the pre-laying shed, the frame or open box is then filled with 3 to 4 inches (7.6–10 cm) of moistened sphagnum moss. When the time is right, most females will lay their clutch and coil within the nest box to brood their eggs. The room or the enclosure should be maintained at a temperature of 84°F–87°F (29°C–30.5°C). It is important not to keep the female too

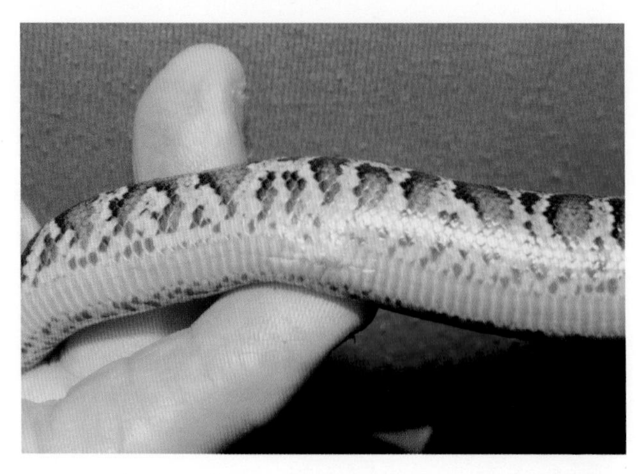

This Burmese hatchling's umbilical scar is still visible.

warm and to provide a temperature range that will allow her to regulate incubation temperature. Female Burmese pythons can through "shivering" and other behaviors raise the temperature within their coils several degrees above the ambient air temperature. However, a female can do little to cool down eggs when the temperature is too high.

A problem that develops when allowing maternal incubation involves the possible dehydration of the eggs. Typically, breeders use a hand sprayer to daily mist the snake and eggs with a thorough spraying of the moss. Some breeders strategically place pieces of clear plastic over the eggs or snake (or both) to reduce the evaporative rate. Increasing the relative humidity of the room with a humidifier is beneficial. Allowing maternal brooding is not recommended with females that appear too thin following egg-laying because a female will not feed during the entire incubation period, which lasts approximately two months.

Artificial Incubation

Another method used by many breeders is to remove the eggs following laying and place them in an incubator maintained at 88°F–90°F (31°C–32°C). A widely used type of incubator is an aquarium with shallow water just a few inches above a submersible heater that has been placed on the floor of the aquarium. With the help of an aquarium thermometer, the heater is calibrated to heat the water to the desired temperature (additional adjustments will have to be made later). Above the water area, a platform is constructed using Plexiglas, bricks, or welded wire on which the container of eggs is placed.

The container in which the python eggs are placed is filled with 2 to 3 inches (5–7.6 cm) of moistened vermiculite (equal parts of water and vermiculite by weight) and the eggs are placed on their sides on top of the vermiculite. Inside the container, a small vessel of water (e.g., a small jar with water) should be added to help maintain a high relative air humidity. The container is then covered with the lid, which should be perforated with a few holes to allow for air exchange. A thermometer should be placed in the container.

One type of thermometer that is very effective for incubators is an electronic digital readout thermometer with outdoor sensors; this type is commonly sold in electronics supply stores. Simply place the sensor probe inside the container and switch the thermometer to the outside reading. This will give you a continuous reading of the temperature inside the container. A backup aquarium thermometer in the water and against the glass should be used; electronic thermometers do occasionally fail.

Place the container on the platform inside the incubator and cover the aquarium with a glass or Plexiglas cover allowing a very small (quarter inch, [6 mm]) open space for air exchange. Some herpetoculturists make a Styrofoam cover to provide better insulation. Over the next few hours carefully monitor the temperature inside the container and, using small adjustments, calibrate the submersible heater until the desired temperature is achieved. Do not neglect calibration of the incubator. If the temperature becomes too high, you could end up cooking your eggs. Proper calibration will take time, so resign yourself to it. On the other hand, once the incubator is calibrated, it can be used in the future with little or no further adjustments. The temperature should be monitored at least twice daily. The eggs should be monitored and examined briefly at least twice a week. They will hatch in approximately two months (fifty-seven to sixty-three days).

Infertile eggs are also called mummies.

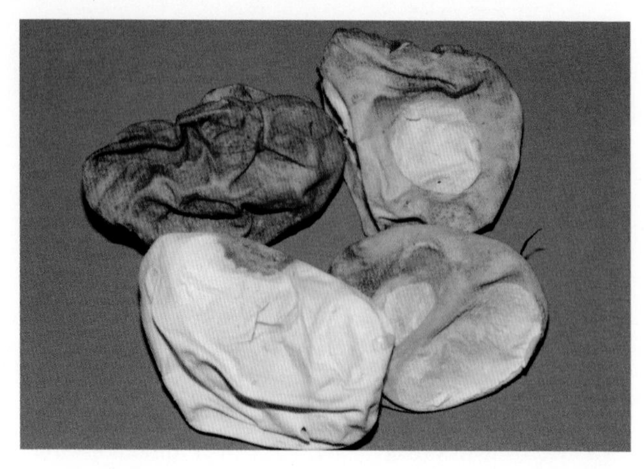

A widely used alternative to homemade incubators are poultry incubators large enough to accommodate the egg containers. These have thermostatic controls that allow one to easily keep the incubation temperature at the desired range.

CHAPTER 6

DISEASES AND DISORDERS

By Roger Klingenberg, DVM

Aside from size considerations, providing health care for Burmese pythons is relatively easy, as they are considered to be hardy captive snakes. Most Burmese are voracious eaters, don't mind being handled, and easily adapt to very basic cage conditions (thriving even in cages without hiding places). However, one husbandry practice that is essential for their long-term health management is that of heat provision.

Burmese pythons will continue to thrive in mildly substandard heat with otherwise good care, but a chronic or dramatic lack of heat will suppress their immune systems, leading to the emergence of a variety of health issues. If symptoms are noted in the early stages of disease and proper treatment provided, the prognosis is better than with most species of snakes maintained for breeding, exhibit, or as pets.

Inclusion Body Disease

Inclusion Body Disease (IBD) is a retrovirus infection (as is AIDS) in which boa constrictors are considered to be the primary host. Burmese pythons are extremely susceptible to infection by these viruses, and exposure in the past led to a dramatic death within weeks, usually characterized by severe neurological signs including tremors, seizures, loss of vision, inability to right themselves when turned over, and inability to control its tongue, prior to succumbing to the virus. The classic reptile literature refers to the condition as

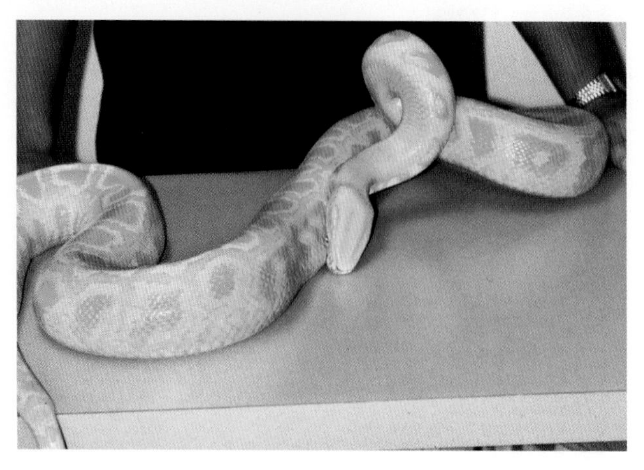

This albino Burmese python exhibits neurological signs consistent with IBD. When placed upside down, the snake could not right itself. In normal positioning the snake would act as if it were blind, off balance, and unable to correct abnormal positioning.

"stargazing syndrome," which is opisthotonus, or a contortion of the neck commonly seen in snakes affected by IBD.

It is interesting to note that over the last two decades Burmese pythons may be developing some immunity or at least defenses to the virus. Whereas certain neurological death used to occur with exposure to IBD, some Burmese now present with a severe, chronic respiratory infection that, while difficult to treat, doesn't always bring certain death. Exposure to this virus occurs with a transfer of infected fluids from other infected snakes by mites, during breeding, and by co-habitation with infected specimens. Considering a high percentage of boa constrictors are thought to be asymptomatic IBD carriers, these snakes should never be mixed with pythons when caged.

Burmese Disease

Burmese Disease (BD) is the common name for a particularly vexing syndrome that breeders have been dealing with for many years. While affecting primarily Burmese pythons, similar symptoms have also been seen in African rock, blood, and Borneo short-tailed pythons that were exposed to affected Burmese pythons. Breeders have noted that symptoms are rarely noted in snakes less than thirty months of age, which clouds the issue of whether younger snakes are not affected or are simply latent carriers that break with the disease after a certain period of time. The typical symptoms of BD are repeated bouts of pneumonia characterized by thick, tenacious phlegm. *Pseudomonas* sp. bacteria are often cultured from the respiratory tract, and in the initial stages the infection responds to antibiotics. However, the respiratory infections tend to recur, and eventually death by asphyxiation occurs. Typical necropsy findings include obstruction of the trachea by thick globs of mucus and bacteria; primarily *Pseudomonas* sp. can be cultured from the secretions. Dave Barker, a renowned and very experienced breeder of Burmese pythons, feels that large losses of snakes from BD are responsible for the crash in the breeding and popularity of these snakes.

At this time, no definitive information about causative agents or transmission is known. It has been reported that veterinary researchers noted that lesions in the lungs of snakes with BD, when examined by electron microscopy, resembled those typical of retrovirus. The facts that this disease is slow, progressive, and characterized by recurrent episodes and involvement of opportunistic bacteria (*Pseudomonas*) strongly suggest immune suppression or compromise. Could this be due to one of the known or a new strain of retrovirus (IBD)? Perhaps the Burmese pythons have developed immune defenses that can hold a retrovirus, or another strain of virus, at bay only to succumb as the snakes mature and age.

Only continued research and repeated necropsy and pathological testing of affected snakes and tissue will provide answers. For the time being, affected snakes should be strictly quarantined and euthanasia should be considered.

Respiratory Disease (Pneumonia)

Respiratory disease is invariably due to significant immune suppression as with exposure to IBD, but much more commonly due to an inadequate heat gradient. In the early stages a respiratory infection may be noted as a noisy, gurgling or "wheezing" type of breathing that is more prominent when the snake is handled. Open-mouthed breathing and elevation of the head are observed as the disease progresses and secretions form and make breathing more diffi-

Copious secretions are noted in the glottis of this python affected with a respiratory infection.

cult. Visualization of a foamy secretion from the mouth and pouching of the lower throat region means the disease is advanced and needs to be treated as soon as possible. The pouching or distention of the pharyngeal region is due to the fact that snakes do not have a diaphragm to help them breathe or cough; the snake is employing the muscles of the throat to aid in respiration. In the very early stages, many pythons will respond to the simple provision of an adequate heat gradient. A reptile veterinarian, who will likely employ systemic antibiotics and nebulization, should evaluate pythons exhibiting open-mouthed breathing.

Stomatitis (Mouth Rot)

Mouth rot is characterized by the accumulation of caseous (cheese-like) pus, mucoid secretions, and necrotic tissue in the mouth and occasionally extending into the throat. This disease entity may occur by itself or in conjunction with other infections such as respiratory or skin diseases, again as a reflection of a suppressed immune system. Treatment consists of providing a proper heat gradient, gently debriding pus and necrotic tissue daily, and the application of both a topical and systemic antibiotic. The fact that a Burmese python is eating doesn't preclude the possibility of oral lesions, but in severe cases feeding will not voluntarily occur until lesions resolve.

Blister Disease and Necrotizing Dermatitis

Infections of the scales with symptoms ranging from mild hemorrhage to severe blistering and ulceration tend to arise from two different scenarios.

Inadequate cage hygiene with accumulation of urates, feces, and excessive moisture can cause primary skin lesions in snakes that cannot avoid contact with this soiled substrate. Such exposure causes a mild chemical burn that is manifest initially as small vesicles or blisters but progresses into ulceration and death of tissue as bacteria take advantage of the compromised tissue. This progression is referred to as blister disease.

Necrotizing dermatitis (scale rot) is a bacterial infection that starts from the inside and works its way out, once again the manifestation of a suppressed immune system. This helps to explain why animals maintained in pristine conditions can still develop skin lesions if husbandry practices do not support the immune system. Once husbandry techniques have been reviewed and corrected (if warranted), treatment consists of gentle debridement of dead tissue, application of a topical antibiotic, systemic antibiotics, and use of a non-adherent substrate such as newspaper. Tissue that has been deeply ulcerated may take several weeks to heal, and scales that are damaged through their full thickness will not regenerate, but are replaced with scar tissue.

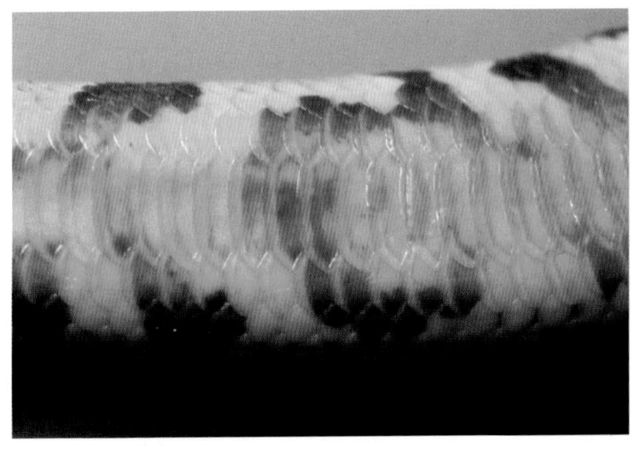

The superficial vesicles and hemorrhages are characteristic of both blister disease and scale rot. Blister disease occurs primarily due to severely inadequate hygiene, and scale rot due to a breakdown of the immune system. It is possible for these syndromes to co-exist.

Parasitism

As the vast majority of Burmese pythons kept in captivity now originate from captive breeding, parasitism is unusual but sometimes seen. Snakes that originate from wild-caught stock may have a wide range of parasites. This author recommends that every captive reptile have fecal examinations performed. Nematode parasites are easily treated with oral fenbendazole (Panacur) at 50 mg orally for three straight days; this regimen is repeated in a week. Cestodes are treated with praziquantel (Droncit) at 5 mg/kg either orally or injected, and then repeated in two weeks. Protozoal infections are treated with metronidazole (Flagyl) at 20 mg/kg orally every forty-eight hours for three to five doses.

External parasites, primarily snake mites, are important to treat due to their potential role as vectors of IBD.

Reproductive Disorders

Burmese pythons can produce prodigious numbers of eggs depending on their age, size, and nutritional status. Owners who are breeding their pythons need to review the Breeding chapter by de Vosjoli and diligently attend to husbandry practices.

Reproduction is a luxury that is afforded only those snakes that are healthy and well-maintained and should be avoided in sick or poorly performing individuals. Once a python has laid a clutch of eggs and the eggs have been removed for incubation, the snake should be carefully examined. The snake should be thoroughly palpated to make sure all the eggs have passed. Normal feeding and other behaviors should resume within a couple of weeks. A reptile veterinarian may perform X rays or ultrasound examinations to make certain that no eggs are retained.

Gastrointestinal Problems

Regurgitation is not common in Burmese pythons and usually is a consequence of large meals without adequate heat to digest the prey item. Regurgitation that continues after correcting husbandry issues often is treated with an antibiotic for a potential gastroenteritis. Trimethoprim/sulfa is often used at 30 mg/kg orally every forty-eight hours as needed. Persistent regurgitation should be evaluated with appropriate diagnostic tests such as fecal samples, CBC/blood chemistry panels, stomach washes, X ray, ultrasound, biopsies, and exploratory surgery.

Constipation is the result of feeding frozen prey items, poor hydration, and, most commonly, a lack of exercise. Prey items that are frozen and thawed lose fluid content and contribute to poor hydration or even dehydration in the animal that eats them. While hydrating fluids such as Gatorade can be injected into prey items, it is easier to provide a soaking container for the snake to use once or twice a week depending on the severity of the problem. Exercising the snake (for example, letting it crawl up or down stairs) at least twice weekly will also stimulate normal peristalsis. Constipation is more than just an issue of comfort; retained uric acid crystals can form into urate balls that irritate or abrade the intestinal lining.

Salmonellosis

Fowl-fed pythons are being exposed to *Salmonella* sp. and other bacteria that cause salmonellosis. Healthy individuals, while not always adversely affected, can become chronic, asymptomatic carriers. Poorly maintained and immunosuppressed individuals can easily become symptomatic carriers. Proper diagnosis requires the services of a veterinarian.

CHAPTER 7

HOW ACCIDENTS HAPPEN

When maintained in a responsible manner and properly handled, Burmese pythons are relatively safe and predictable animals. The same can be said of dogs, yet every year millions of dollars are spent in the treatment of dog bites and ten to fifteen people are killed by dogs.

The most common misconception with captive-raised Burmese is that they are tame and, therefore, will not demonstrate aggressive behavior toward humans, such as biting or constricting, because they can recognize humans as harmless. This may be true under most circumstances, but nothing changes the fact that Burmese pythons are not very smart creatures and that they are very large snakes with interpretational systems characteristic of snakes—not humans. Don't test them.

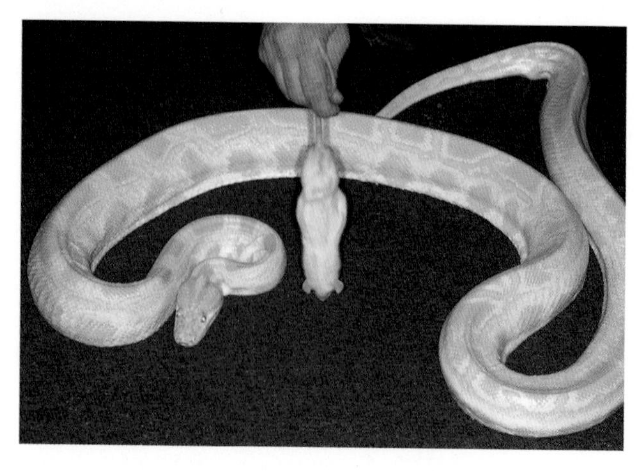

This is an easy way for an accident to happen. A snake likely won't differentiate between your arm and the prey you dangle in front of its face. Be smart—use tools such as tongs to encourage a snake to accept prey if it doesn't readily feed on its own.

Causes of Common Accidents

- Poor feeding practices: This includes offering or removing prey animals by hand, leading to accidental biting and constricting. Another common cause of accidents involves opening a cage to pick up a Burmese python after you have been recently handling rats or rabbits while feeding other snakes. Pythons recognize prey animals primarily by scent. If that hand doesn't look like a rabbit but sure smells like one, then by God it must be fair prey. Oops.
- Allowing a Burmese python to form a complete loop around one's neck: Under certain circumstances, such as simply by tightening its muscles to retain its balance, a large constrictor can apply enough pressure to lead to temporary suffocation and stop blood flow to the brain, possibly resulting in loss of consciousness. Have an assistant present to assist with handling large snakes.
- Unconsciously establishing undesirable behavioral associations: If you've ignored your pet Burmese for the last three months because you've had to put in extra hours at your job and the only time you open its cage is to toss in the rabbit, you are unconsciously conditioning your snake to expect food and to be prepared to strike every time you open the cage.

  Don't be surprised, therefore, if after three months without any handling, you open up the cage to pick up your pet and get nailed. Many people establish behaviors associated with handling prior to picking up a snake. Some use a snake stick to move the forward part of the body and gently stroke the snake before picking it up. Others will cover the head with a piece of cloth and gently stroke the back of their snake before picking it up.

  A lot will depend on the routines that you establish. If your snake is fed well and if you regularly take it out for handling, it will not necessarily associate the opening of the door with feeding. Think carefully about the associations you are creating.

Bites

The standard defensive behavior of all large constrictors including Burmese pythons is to strike, bite, and quickly release. Initially, all hatchling Burmese pythons have a low threshold for defensive behavior, but within a relatively short period of time and with regular handling this behavioral propensity should gradually subside. Though, like people, all Burmese pythons are not created alike. There will be those individuals that remain nervous and restless when handled. Some of these individuals will be unpredictable and occasionally strike out and bite. There will also be those uptight few that persist in their nastiness to the point that they will grow into perfectly predictable nippy adults. Besides aggression, most people are bitten by Burmese pythons as a result of poor feeding practices. In most cases, bites can be prevented by adopting better herpetocultural practices.

The consequences of Burmese python bites will vary in direct relation to size. A bite from a hatchling Burmese will inflict pinpoint punctures and lacerations that will be somewhat painful but of no great or lasting consequence. On the other hand, an adult Burmese python can inflict deep lacerations and multiple puncture wounds with much more serious consequences. Many factors can contribute to the severity of the bite, particularly whether the bitten individual pulls back when the bite is inflicted or the snake pulls back while the teeth remain imbedded in the wounds. Under certain circumstances, a bad bite from an adult Burmese python can require stitches and result in scars. Bites by large pythons also tend to readily become infected.

A gentle Burmese with a good disposition is very unlikely to bite, but some can be so predictably nasty that necessary precautions should be taken whenever they are handled. The worst cases involving bites often are associated with bad feeding practices that result in a bite followed by constriction, such as the dummy who dangled a prekilled rabbit by the scruff of the neck in front of his large Burmese to incite it to strike. He ended up with 14 feet (4.3 m) of python holding on with God knows how many teeth imbedded in his hand. The snake retained its hold, constricting more and more as the "prey" just kept on moving. With sound herpetocultural practices, bites by Burmese pythons can easily be prevented.

Watch That Tail!

Some Burmese are so nasty that handling them requires either the use of a snake stick and holding the tail or, in cases where medical treatment might be necessary, grabbing the snake behind the head and holding the rest of the body. (A second person should be present with any large snake greater than 8 feet [2.4 m] when performing this procedure.) Under these circumstances, nasty or nervous Burmese have a knack for expelling copious amounts of urates and foul-smelling musk. Sometimes they may also defecate, so watch that tail and hold it in such a way that you don't get "sprayed." The end result could be smeared and smelly clothes that will require changing. Furthermore, you will stink and will need to take a shower.

Constriction

Problems involving constriction usually result either from feeding two snakes in the same cage (one constricts the other while both are trying to feed on the same prey item) or the very rare circumstances where a human is involved.

In the first case, the easy solution is to prevent it. Never feed two large snakes together in the same cage. The result can be skin and eye injuries, broken ribs, and damage to internal organs. If faced with this problem, assuming that you are a responsible herpetoculturist and have a friend nearby when the snakes involved are more than 8 feet (2.4 m) long, each person should simply grab a snake behind the head and try to get the most easily removed one to release its grip. Unwind at least one of them, keeping a hold behind the head, and place it in a separate cage. Next time, don't feed them in the same cage.

In the very rare case of a human or part of a human (an arm is often involved) constricted by a snake, the procedure is the same but speed may be critical. If the head is placed such that it can't be made to easily release its grip, then unwind by the tail end. You can deal with the head later.

CHAPTER 8

NOTES ON OTHER LARGE PYTHONS

Indian Python, *Python molurus molurus*

The species *Python molurus* has been called by some the Asiatic rock python, with two subspecies, the Burmese python (*P. m. bivittatus*) and the Indian python (*P. m. molurus*). The most obvious distinguishing feature of the Indian python is the attractive light coloration compared with the Burmese. Another feature is that the lance-shaped mark on top of the head usually is distinct only posteriorly, to the level of the eyes (it reaches toward the tip of the snout in the Burmese). If uncertain whether you have a pure Indian or an Indian x Burmese hybrid, a useful character involves the scalation beneath the eyes—in pure Indians the sixth or

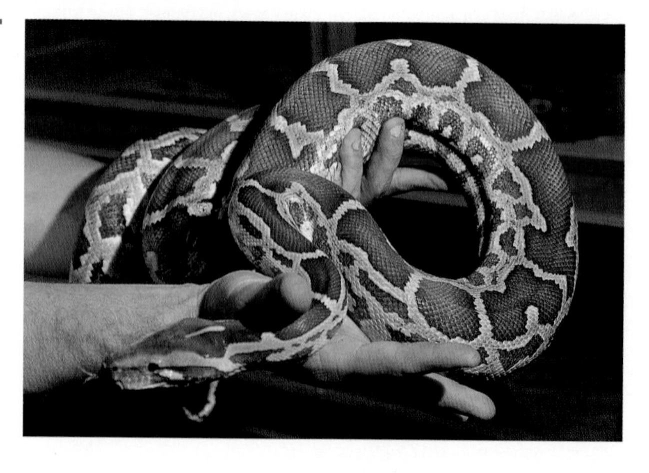

Indian rock pythons (*P. m. molurus*) are usually lighter in color compared with Burmese pythons.

seventh upper labial (lip scale) usually will reach the edge of the eye, while in Burmese the labials are separated from the eye by a row of small subocular scales.

Distribution

Western Pakistan to Nepal and all of India

Protection

Because the United States lists it as endangered under the Endangered Species Act (ESA), this subspecies cannot be sold or transported between states without a special permit from the U.S. Fish and Wildlife Service. An unfortunate consequence of this regulation has been a trend toward hybridizing Indian with Burmese pythons to avoid the hassles of red tape, etc.

Temperament

While many authors have raved about the docile personality of Indian pythons, in the author's experience Burmese pythons as a whole are more docile than most of the Indian pythons currently offered in the trade.

Maintenance

General care and feeding requirements are similar to those of Burmese pythons.

Breeding

Again, Indian pythons are bred much like Burmese pythons, but they usually breed at an older age and are not as reliable or consistent as Burmese pythons.

Sri Lankan Python, *P. molurus pimbura*

Though the Sri Lankan python is now often considered as just a variety of *Python molurus molurus* (which means that U.S. Fish and Wildlife could now consider it as an Appendix I, ESA. animal like the Indian python), most herpetoculturists believe this to be a sufficiently distinct form to warrant its recognition as a separate subspecies...but herpetoculturists are not herpetologists. The Sri Lankan python is

The Sri Lankan python (or the Ceylon python) (*P. m. pimbura*) has a beautiful high-contrast pattern but a nasty disposition.

nonetheless a markedly different insular form of *P. molurus* characterized by a distinctive high-contrast pattern, more prominent eyes, subtle morphological differences, and consistently more aggressive temperament that make it unmistakable from the mainland Indian python.

Sri Lankan pythons are currently bred by relatively few herpetoculturists. As a rule, they are the least docile of the *molurus* complex. In fact, most of the Sri Lankan pythons currently bred and offered for sale in the United States rank among the nastiest pythons one is likely to encounter. Regular handling from the time they are hatchlings will have relatively little effect on the temperament of these animals. At best they will grow into consistently unreliable adults. These are attractive animals in their own right, but if you are looking for a pet, this would probably not be a very good choice. Maintenance and breeding are similar to the Indian python, but it does not breed as readily.

Reticulated Python, *Python reticulatus*

Twenty years ago the notion that reticulated pythons could ever achieve any degree of popularity would have been inconceivable. They had the reputation of growing large and nasty. This was in part because of the age and larger size of imported wild-collected animals, typically 3 feet (91 cm) or more, most of which originated from Thailand. Currently, reticulated pythons rank among those highest in demand of

The reticulated python (*P. reticulatus*) tiger morph's popularity is not only due to its bold striped pattern, but also to its docility relative to other retics.

the giant snakes. Their popularity is due to several factors. The first is that increasing numbers of reticulated pythons were bred in captivity, and when raised from hatchlings many became as tame as Burmese pythons. The second is the advent of the tiger reticulated python, a large morph characterized by reduced background pattern with striping. Tiger retics demonstrated an unusual docility compared to typical retics, with some individuals showing a greater degree of responsiveness toward their owners than just about any other snake species. The third has been the availability of albino reticulated pythons, arguably the most beautiful snakes in the world. The fourth has been the influx of imports from Indonesia, notably of dwarf morphs that

This super tiger reticulated morph shows even more defined striping than seen in regular tiger morphs.

Uncoiled, this adult reticulated python reaches 18 feet long.

grow slowly and can remain less than 12 feet (3.6 m). Because of all the above, the reticulated python has become a snake lover's archetype, combining manageable size, extreme beauty, and potential for great docility. The reticulated python is living art in progress, with breeders combining several morphs in the goal of creating smaller snakes with extreme beauty and nice temperament.

In spite of these qualities, most specimens and morphs of the reticulated python remain large snakes and will require a great commitment of time, space, and labor to house and maintain responsibly. As with any large animal, whether a horse or large dog breed, reticulated pythons are not for everyone.

The reticulated python is considered by many as one of the most intelligent of all snakes, but there is enough variation in this widely distributed species and its many populations that making generalizations is difficult. Some retics are bite-prone, some are unpredictable, others can be very tame, and a few can shows signs of intelligence and what one could call a degree of owner recognition and responsiveness.

I can talk about this subject because in the late 1960s I visited a well-known snake-keeper in Florida who had raised a reticulated python from a hatchling, initially carrying it in her pocket and later even allowing it to sleep in her bed. At the time, I was with my friend Mike Mittleman, and we were told to enter a mobile home. We were then asked to sit on the floor of a large room with several free-roaming large constrictors including a 20+-foot (6+ m) reticulated python. "Stay still and let him check you out," we were told. The beast came over and investigated us. It had the largest head we had ever seen on snake, like a large dog's, and it ran its head over us, including our faces, tongue-flicking repeatedly as we sat as still as mummies. We apparently passed some type of test because the snake eventually turned and crawled away.

Later, its owner held a demonstration of this python's ability to recognize individuals. At one point half its body was in one room and the other in the hallway and part way in another room. She asked us to come with her where the tail end was. "Pet it," she told us. As we ran a hand along its back, the python made the kind of aversive full-body twitch snakes will sometimes make when they are feeding and another snake makes contact with them. We repeated the experiment; it twitched again. Then its owner proceeded to pet the snake and it remained calm. We later read that this female python would coil around its owner and brood her as if she were a clutch of eggs. I have heard other stories of signs of owner recognition and "bonding" involving other retics kept in room-sized enclosures, notably tiger reticulated pythons.

Although this type of story might seem to encourage the ownership of these snakes, the degree of commitment and time and the price that one pays for testing these limits of

Prior snake-keeping experience is recommended for those interested in purchasing reticulated pythons. Adult specimens, such as the one shown here, can reach lengths up to 20 or more feet (typically in females; males reach about 14 feet).

human-snake interrelationships are often great, can be risky, and have harmful effects on social relationships and other aspects of your life. Anyone who spends an inordinate amount of time "relating" with their pet snake will likely be considered eccentric if not downright nutty. You must also realize that in some cases misinterpretation of behaviors can lead to serious injury or death. However, these interactions do suggest possibilities of domestication that make you wonder where research on possible imprinting and selective breeding for intelligence and tameness could lead.

Distribution

This widely distributed species of python is found in Southeast Asia, peninsular Malaysia, and many of the islands of the Philippines and Indonesia.

Size

Depending on morph, sex, and environmental conditions, reticulated pythons can range from 6 feet (1.8 m) (dwarf males) to 20+ feet (6+ m) (large females). Males of typical *P. reticulatus* generally reach 10 to 14 feet (3–4.2 m). Females will typically grow to at least 16 feet (4.8 m) and can exceed 20 feet (6 m) and weigh more than 250 pounds (more than 112 kg). The record length for the species is nearly 33 feet (9.9 m). With the exception of the dwarf morphs, this is a fast-growing species that can exceed 12 feet (3.6 m) in only two years if raised under an intensive feeding regimen.

Selection

It cannot be emphasized enough that you should always plan to see large retics and their housing in person, either at zoos, at specialized stores, or in private collections prior to purchase. These are powerful, heavy-duty snakes only recommended for individuals with prior experience keeping larger snakes and who can provide the conditions required. Plan on the space you aim to make available for caging a large specimen prior to purchase of even a juvenile, and make sure you line up a food source. You must absolutely have a secure enclosure with a proper locking mechanism.

Hobbyists now have a great range of choices when considering buying a reticulated python, and I can't emphasize enough that you should carefully study the subject and search the Web sites of breeders, examine photos, and evaluate the potential size of the various morphs. Note that male reticulated pythons grow significantly smaller than females (about 40 percent shorter and a third of the weight) and may be a more manageable choice for many hobbyists. If your plan is to breed reticulated pythons, you should carefully evaluate the market. At the present time, the primary goal of specialized breeders appears to be to establish dwarf forms of tigers and albinos, which will require several generations of selective breeding. With retics, size should definitely be a consideration. Like Burmese pythons, retics can quickly grow to a size where they can no longer be easily lifted, moved, or maintained by a single person. As with other giant snakes, another person should always be present during maintenance. For the great majority of prospective buyers, the recently available dwarf morphs may be the wisest choice when they become more widely available.

Morphs

There are more than a dozen morphs of reticulated pythons currently available in the reptile trade. The following is an overview of the most popular.

Population

There are large numbers of population morphs offered in the current market, including silver-headed, yellow-headed, Sulawesi, and others. If a wild-type reticulated python is what you are looking for, then you should investigate these many morphs, which can vary in terms of appearance and temperament.

Tiger and Super Tiger

The tiger trait is a genetic mutation that produces a reduced pattern including a mostly tan middorsal area, varying degrees of striping, and, in some cases, lateral duplication of the pattern. Part of the black line found on the top of the

Retic tiger morphs such as this juvenile typically are missing part of the black stripe that appears on the heads of reticulated pythons.

head of a typical retic is missing, and the white spots on the sides are enlarged and elongated. The tiger morph was originally obtained and bred by Karl Hermann and later developed by Al and Cindy Baldogo, who determined that it was a co-dominant trait. Because it is codominant, when a tiger is mated to a normal reticulated python, there is a 50 percent probability that the offspring will be tigers and 50 percent probability that they will be normal. When a tiger is mated to a tiger, there is a 25 percent probability of obtaining normals, 50 percent probability of tiger, and 25 percent of a morph called super tiger that has mostly a yellowish to tan background color with thin black stripes. The tiger trait represents the heterozygous condition of the mutation, and the super tiger the homozygous condition.

Tiger reticulated pythons grow large, and descendants of the original line have the reputation of being very docile. Supposedly some outbred lines have not retained the mellow temperament that has made this morph a favorite of large snake breeders.

Albino

There are currently at least three forms of albino reticulated pythons, commonly grouped as white, lavender, and purple. These variants can appear in a clutch of any albino breeding so are probably not alleles of the same albino gene. The albino trait is a simple recessive that can be combined with any of the other genetic morphs, such as the tiger.

Dwarf

These originate from various Indonesian islands including Bali, Kalaota, and islands in the Sunda Islands chain. The Jampea form (and this may apply to other dwarfs in the Sunda Islands chain) was described as a new subspecies, Python reticulatus jampeanus, by Auliya, Mausfeld, Schmitz, and Böhme in 2002. Dwarves grow much more slowly than standard reticulated pythons and, depending on feeding schedules, can remain less than 8 feet (2.4 m) for males and less than 12 feet (3.6 m) for females. It requires three to four years for captive-raised female dwarf retics to reach 7 feet (2.1 m). However, under an intensive feeding regimen even dwarf retics can exceed 12 feet (3.6 m), with one record of a female achieving 15 feet (4.5 m).

The smallest captive-bred line is offered as super dwarfs. Further selective breeding could establish lines that consistently remain less than 10 feet (3 m), possibly smaller. This could result in reticulated pythons that potentially would offer little danger to owners and be more manageable in terms of housing and feeding. It would also make them drop out of the category of giant snakes. The dwarf trait is likely polygenetic, but for practical purposes it is dealt with as if it were a codominant trait (it isn't). When crossed with normal size retics, the result is a range of sizes, most of which will be intermediate between dwarf and normal.

Maintenance

Care and feeding requirements of the reticulated python are generally similar to those of Burmese pythons of similar size.

Breeding

Retics breed in a fashion similar to Burmese pythons but are less consistent than Burmese pythons. They can breed as early as two years but often will not breed until four years or more. Reticulated pythons usually do not breed every year. Cooling to the mid 70s F in early fall is usually sufficient to induce breeding later in the fall. Close attention must be given to the ambient temperature if maternal incubation is allowed because of the limited ability of reticulated pythons to raise their body temperature. In captivity, eggs incubated at 88°F–90°F (about 32°C) require about ninety days to hatch.

African Rock Pythons, *Python sebae* and *Python natalensis*

Currently African pythons constitute two species: the Central African rock python (*P. sebae*), which is the third largest species of snake and can grow to more than 25 feet (7.5 m); and the smaller South African rock python (*P. natalensis*), recently elevated to a full species and said to grow to only 9 (males) to 15 feet (females) (2.7–4.5 m). The two species can be distinguished by differences in head scalation and pattern. *P. natalensis* has the frontal scales broken into two to seven scales and lacks the well-defined large dark blotch in front of the eye that is found in *P. sebae*; the subocular blotch is reduced to a dark streak.

These species are currently kept and bred by a few specialist breeders and are of interest only to a small number of large snake aficionados. Although attractive and interesting in their own right, they are less colorful than some and have the reputation of being aggressive. However, like many reticulated pythons, some can become quite tame when raised from captive-bred hatchlings. Much of what has been said about reticulated pythons applies to these species.

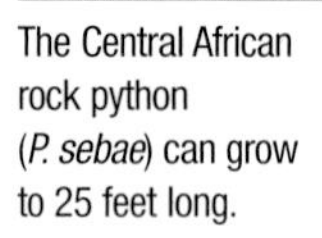

The Central African rock python (*P. sebae*) can grow to 25 feet long.

The South African rock python (*P. natalensis*) is of a smaller size (up to 15 feet in females) and lacks the well-defined dark blotch in front of the eye commonly seen in the Central African rock python.

Size

Hatchlings of *P. sebae* average about 2 feet (61 cm). Adults are typically 11 to 18 feet (3.3–5.4 m) long. The largest specimens of *P. sebae* are from West Africa. The record is nearly 32 feet (9.6 m).

Longevity

These are long-lived snakes. There is a record of an African rock python having lived at the San Diego Zoo for twenty-seven years and four months.

Morphs

The wild-type morph is now seldom bred in captivity, but patternless, striped, and hypomelanistic (reduced dark pigment) morphs have been established by Jay Brewer of Prehistoric Pets. Some of his patternless and hypomelanistic morphs have an attractive golden background, and his lines have the reputation of being tame and easy to manage.

Maintenance

These snakes grow very large, and their care requirements are generally the same as for reticulated pythons. This species will not hesitate to climb on large tree branches at night. Some specimens will be consistently tame, but others will be unpredictable and prone to biting.

Breeding

Investigate the market before breeding these snakes. The current market for African rock pythons is very small and will likely remain so. Their breeding requirements are generally identical to reticulated pythons. Under optimal rearing conditions they can achieve sexual onset by two years and about 6 feet (1.8 m) for males and three to four years and 9 to 10 feet (2.7–3 m) for females. They should be cooled in the fall with night temperatures allowed to drop about 10°F (about 5°C) down to the mid 70s F. A female should be introduced to the male's enclosure at regular intervals during this period until mating has been witnessed. Mating occurs in late fall through winter. Clutch size numbers from twenty to more than eighty eggs depending on the size of the female. The eggs hatch in seventy to eighty days at an incubation temperature of 88°F–90°F (about 32°C).

RESOURCES

Barker, D. 1990. One of a kind. *Vivarium* 2(6): 32–33.

Clark, B. 1988. Breeding the albino Burmese python. *Vivarium* 1(1): 18–21.

———. 1996. Python color and pattern morphs. *Reptiles* 4(3): 56–67.

———. 1997. Tiger, tiger… *Vivarium* 8(4) 37.

———. 2000. Big & beautiful. *Reptiles* 8(1): 52–61.

Frye, F. 1981. *Biomedical and Surgical Aspects of Captive Reptile Husbandry.* Melbourne, Fla.: Krieger.

Ross, R. A. and G. Marzec. 1991. *The Reproductive Husbandry of Pythons and Boas.* Stanford, Calif.: Institute for Herpetological Research.

Wagner, E. 1976. Breeding the Burmese python *Python molurus bivittatus* at Seattle Zoo. I*nternational Zoo Yearbook* 16: 83–85.

Wagner, E. and D. Richardson. 1989. A safe, practical python facility. *Proc. 13th International Herpetological Symposium on Captive Propagation and Husbandry*: 111–112. Hawthorne, NJ: IHS, Inc.

INDEX

ABOUT THE AUTHORS

Philippe de Vosjoli was born in 1949 in Paris, France. When in his teens, he was introduced to naturalistic vivarium design by an eccentric former keeper at the Jardin des Plantes.

Since that time he has become the herpetocultural pioneer who founded the first nationally distributed reptile and amphibian magazine, *The Vivarium*, and the best-selling Advanced Vivarium Systems™ line of reptile care books. His many articles and books have established many of the standards used in the field today, including popularizing terms such as "herpetoculture" and "vivarium."

In 1995, he was awarded the Josef Laszlo Memorial Award for Excellence in Herpetoculture and for his contribution to the advancement of the field. He is currently working on developing a systems approach to keeping amphibians and reptiles that focuses on the aesthetic and functional aspects of naturalistic vivaria.

Roger Klingenberg, DVM, is a graduate of Colorado State University Veterinary School. He is a well-known author, speaker, and researcher on herpetoculture and herpetological medicine and surgery and has authored dozens of papers, articles, and text chapters on these topics. He is the author of *Understanding Reptile Parasites*, the popular best-seller in herpetological medicine. He is the founder, owner, and senior veterinarian of a busy veterinary practice that serves small and exotic pets and is an active member of the Association of Amphibian and Reptile Veterinarians. Dr. Klingenberg is probably best known for his collaborations with Philippe de Vosjoli, having coauthored several texts including *The Box Turtle Manual*, *The Boa Constrictor Manual*, and others.